SISTER FM DIVA

POETRY INNA MI YAHD

Verna Hampton

UNCLE B.
PUBLICATIONS

Indianapolis, Indiana

The poem Michelle's Arms was first presented at the Poetry Electric series After Colored Girl 'Cause the Rainbow Ain't Enough at La MaMa, February 18, 2013 in New York City. It was first published in the Palgrave Macmillan Anthology Michelle Obama's Impact on African American Women and Girls in 2018.

The poem Rap To The Rag Trade was written in response to a 1997 incident at a Century 21 store in the Wall Street area of New York City. The incident involved five members of the Henry Street Settlement/ Abrams Art Center's Cultural Harmony theater company.

Table Of Contents

Where Do I Come From

Where do I come from?
I come from Africa.
        I come from Boston.
                I come from Brooklyn.

I come from stolen displaced Africans brought here on ships
and sold to a man named Yopp.
I also come from the Yopps.

I come from Tobe, Alverine, Zula, Big Red, Staples, Elaine, Blaque
Jack,
A light skinned Pullman Porter and a dark skinned Navy man.

I come from a Momma who was very 'hankty' very 'siditty'
But she could get down to the Do Wah Ditty.

I come from a mother who told me 'You are a Princess'
And nuns who called me 'you people'

I come from my guts...I come from my heart.

I come from St. John's, St. Ann's, St Hughes, and The Blessed Sacra-
ment Convent
For Negroes
And Indians.

I come from Down South Georgia and Up South Massachusetts.
Louise Day Hicks and Lester Maddox.
Sardis, Vidalia, Savannah, Valdosta. Roxbury, Dorchester, Mattapan.

I come from fried chicken, collard greens, and potato salad... Five
dollars a plate.

The Odessa and Leshkos on Avenue A.
Pierogis, blintzes and real mashed potatoes.
Papa Leroy's home cooked Navy meals.
And Granny Wright's cakes...made from scratch.

I come from coq au vin, lasagna, bagels, steak, salad baked beans,
Corn on the cob lobster, hog maws chitlins
And fried fish on Fridays

I come from Hallelujah...Shalom...Thank you Jesus...Allah u Akbar.

I come from Patricia Flannery, Richard Mirowski, Constance DeBella
Old Eastern European men sitting in the Bialystoker delicatessen
On Blue Hill Avenue, drinking tea from a glass.
And Zelda's mother...Who had numbers on her arm.

I come from my guts...I come from my heart

I come from "We Shall Overcome", Free Breakfast for Children...
School Busing
The Honorable Elijah Muhammed, JFK, Fred Hampton,
Malcolm X, Medgar Evers, Emmitt Till, Dr. Martin Luther King
And "Up Against the Wall Motherfucker... Take Your Boot Off My
Neck Or I'll Snatch Your Leg Off."

I come from...If you take the A train or
The J train or the 1,2,3,
The Four Tops, Aretha, The Temptations,
The 1812 Overture
Ooh baby baby...there's a PARTY TONIGHT...
It's Howdy Doody time; Turn that music down!
And Nina Simone…
I wish you knew how it would feel to be me
And everybody knows about Mississippi Goddam!!!

I come from Katherine Dunham, Maria Tallchief, Shirley Chisolm, Professor Mahoney, Mrs. Sullivan, Hattie McDaniel, Paul Robeson, Dorothy Dandridge, Nikki Giovanni, Susan Batson, Marvin Felix 'Pancho' Camillo, Robbie McCauley, Maestro Barry Harris, Dr. Elma Lewis, Queen Mother Moore, Ruby Bridges, Fannie Lou Hammer, Melnea Cass, Bayard Ruskin, Louis Armstrong, yeah I come from Pops.

I come from my guts...I come from my heart

Where do I come from?
I come from You.

Sister FM Diva Theme Song: Walking To My Own Beat

She's down adventurous voluptuous and alive
She tells it like it is she don't deal in no jive
She brings a message to help us through our lives

She's SISTER FM D. I. V. A.

Turn her on your dial
She can make vexed she can make you smile
She keeps you on the right track
And stay tuned we'll be right back
With Sister FM

D. I. V. A.
D. I. V. A.
D. I. V. A.

Weather Report

Whether the weather be fine
Or whether the weather be not
We'll weather the weather
Whatever the weather, whether we like it or not
Whether it's hurricanes, torrential rains
Hail, tornadoes or droughts
Tsunami waves, the earth that quakes
Volcanoes where hot lava spews out
Global warming, global warming
Is it true...I tell you...what shall we do?
A cool spring a summery fall
And during the winter the temps hardly fall
Oil slicks on the sea
Big business and speculators killing the trees
And there has also been a great shortage of bees
What is the cause, what is the cause
Mother nature is going through forced menopause

AAAAAaaaaaAAAAARGHHHHHH!

Global warming, global warming
Is it true...I tell you...what will we do?
From nuclear war to the man next door
I'll tell you what I'm screaming for
Give a refrain about acid rain
We may never see a live lake again
Global warming, global warming
Is it true...I tell you...what will we do
Give a shout ozone fall-out
Try explaining to the children what that's all about
Burn the chemicals create a wasteland
The fate of the universe is in technology's hand

Give a scream about you and me

About a constitution that says all are free
Well where is the equality? Where is our reality?
Having to be what we are not
Fighting for jobs someone else hasn't got
Thanks amerikkka thanks a lot
For an economy an eek on oh meeeeee
I'm sure it could be the death of you and me
Whether the weather be fine
Or whether the weather be not
We'll weather the weather
Whatever the weather
Whether we like it or not
We've all worked here in this land
Bucket on floor mop in hand
Bowing and scraping and saying yes sir
Saying yes ma'am
Teachers sweatshops
Technos, medicos, laymen
Waiting at the bus stops
Hold onto your wallets tight
And watch out for the next tax rip-off
Did a little piece work
In one hour I made fifteen ninety-nine
World Trade Organization hired a country
And now they cut my time.
Whether the weather be fine
Or whether the weather be not
We'll weather the weather whatever the weather
Whether we like it or not
Whether we like it or not
Whether we like it or not.

Scream

We can't keep our silence
When we're living with violence
We've got to scream
To the politicians
They are aware of the conditions
They are fighting and signing for peace
Throughout the world and in the middle east
But the wars are still raging
In our homes and towns and on our city streets
We can't keep our silence
When we're living with violence
We've got to scream
To the law enforcement agencies
Serve and protect us
Not murder and disrespect us
Get rid of those crooked cops
That will help crime to drop
We can't keep our silence
When we're living with violence
We've got to scream
To our daughters and sons
Teach the children about
Life, the truth, gangs and guns
Teach them to respect and not bully
Their sister and brother
Kill the madness not each other
We can't keep our silence
When we're living with violence
We've got to scream
To the folks in our community
Organize our blocks and strive for unity
Black, Brown, Red, Yellow, White,
Old, young, straight or gay

We have got to work together and in our collective voices say
We can't keep our silence when we're living with violence
We can't keep our silence when we're living with violence
We can't keep our silence when we're living with violence
WE'VE GOT TO SCREAM!!!

World Trade Center: Ten Years Later

The bravest and the boldest
The youngest and the oldest
Black, Brown, Red, Yellow, White
Were taken from our sight
But not out of our Minds
Have you ever really taken the time to think
That we were really on the brink
Of destruction
Our lives became slurpee suction cups
Of malady and mishap
As the powers that be sat in the lap
Of luxury
The bravest and the boldest
The youngest and the oldest
Black, Brown, Red, Yellow, White
Were taken from our sight
But not out of mind
Have you ever really taken the time to think
That we were really on the brink
Of destruction
Toxic cocktails coated our entrails
And we were told we had nothing to fear
Then more wars started
And loved ones departed
Returning home
With physical and emotional tears
Now the cancer, the asthma, the tumors
The day and nightmares
Still continue to attack us
After ten years

Rage On Recidivism

Webster's dictionary: Recidivism is a tendency to relapse into previous condition or mode of behavior; especially relapse into criminal behavior. The tendency of a convicted criminal to reoffend.

Words that rhyme with recidivism: absenteeism, alcoholism, behaviorism, do nothingism, cannibalism, capitalism, commercialism, Hispanicism and Afrocentrism

This information puts me in a rage A RAGE on RECIDIVISM!!!

Recidivism affects personal growth energy!
Recidivism aids and abets gene enslavement!
Recidivism incubates gang empires Rape atrocities, guns, evil!
Recidivism alleviates a good education!
Recidivism aids the government with an incarcerated unpaid workforce
While the private and affluent coffers fill!

Recidivism does not:
Enlighten
        Reclaim
                Achieve

Go forward
        Empower
                Release
                        Allow
                                Growth
                                        Emancipate!

Rap to The Rag Trade

You act like you're afraid of us
When you see us walk in here
And we are wearing baggy jeans
But this is the store where we buy them
Through ads on billboards, on t.v., and in magazines
Don't believe the hype
The type of clothes I wear doesn't make me type
Because I wear a hoodie doesn't make me a hood
The clothes that I put on doesn't make me bad or good

Don't dis me 'cause you may miss me
Don't even try it 'cause we may not buy it

Now when you see a group of B boys
with their B caps turned around
Are you afraid that they may 'Getcha'
Be they red, yellow, black, white or brown?
Baggy pants and untied shoes
Yeah that started in "The Joint"

But then
          folks looked
                        and saw
                                the Style
Now the dollar sign and decimal point
That Mad. Ave put to this fad
Has turned a youth's experience into
something very sad

Don't dis me 'cause you may miss me
Don't even try it 'cause we may not buy it

Because I wear a baldy

Doesn't make me a nazi skinhead or a thug
Because I wear a gold chain
And carry a beeper
Doesn't mean I am selling drugs
Don't believe the hype
The type of clothes I wear
Does not make me a type

Don't dis me 'cause you may miss me
Don't even try it

'Cause we may not buy it
If you want to quell it
Just don't sell it

Gun, Gun, Gun, Gun, Guns

The ballot or the bullet
That's what Brother Malcolm X said
Then the bullets of assassins rang out
And killed El Shabazz dead

Gun, Gun, Gun, Gun, Guns

The revolution has come
It's time to pick up the gun
That's what we in the Black Panther Party sung
We have now turned the guns
On our own communities
And we are killing
Our own mothers, fathers,
Daughters and sons

Gun, Gun, Gun, Gun, Guns

A Midwest teen said
His high school peers
Were mean
Next day
He brought in an uzi
Wiped out the students, the teachers, and the dean

Gun, Gun, Gun, Gun, Guns

A racist bigot sat in a church
On a wooden pew
As the congregation
Of another hue
Prayed
He pulled out his gun and let the bullets spray

Nine innocent Black people were shot and murdered that day

Gun, Gun, Gun, Gun, Guns

Smith & Wesson gets all the cash
And lobbyists on the senate floor.
While children are maimed, killed,
And crippled by bullets
While playing at home, in the park
And in front of their own door.

Gun, Gun, Gun, Gun, Guns

Mr. and Mrs. America kept their gun, for protection
In the closet way up high.
Little Jr. climbed up on the ladder
And reached
BAM BAM BAM
Now he could live or he may die.

GUN GUN GUN GUN, GUN GUN GUN GUN, GUN GUN GUN
GUNNnnnnnnn SSssss.

Everytown Research & Policy 04.27.2021
More than 100 americans are shot and killed per day
More than 230 americans are shot and wounded per day

Open Season For No Reason

Open season for no reason
Other than being Black and free
And everything else everyone wants to be
Oh everybody wants to be me...we'll see!
Open season for no reason
Other than to be
You kidnapped most of us
From our motherland
Put shackles
On our beautiful black hands
Told us that we…
We're not free
But we didn't know anything else to be!
Open season for no reason
Other than it is you and me
We were forced onto these shores
Slavers using our
Tortured bones for oars
And the triangle trade soars
OUR BLOOD
Soaked slave ship decks
Shackles tightly
Screwed around our necks
Open season for no reason
Because of your greed
You committed many an atrocious deed
Throw us into the sea
That is where we would rather be
Than to be kidnapped
And brought to your amerikkkan shores
Open season for no reason
Other than your privileged hate
You sold us at the auction gates

Throughout your
United snakes of amerikkka states
In big cities and in small towns
We made millionaires
And billionaires of many...
Including the washingtons,
The jeffersons, the fanuels,
The dudleys and the browns.
From our backs and our brains
Our torture and pains
The blood, sweat, and tears
You have inflicted upon my mighty people for generations of years
We suckled nursed and raised you
Taken care of from the cradle to the grave
You stole my sweet Nubian babies
And sold them
To have your new roads paved
Open season for no reason
Fast forward to the twenty-first century
We have made many important milestones
In this here land where we be
And You are still oppressing, stressing
Killing, Maiming and Murdering me

Brother Bunchy Carter said it best
"What's there to talk about, we still ain't free"
All Power to The People...Reparations Now

What Is A Name

What is a name what is a name tell me tell me true
The term by which any person is known
To give a name to
What is a name sometimes a name is a family tree
My great grandma had my name first
When I was born her name was given to me.

A name is a tribute to our homeland
Ancestors present future and past
People dedicating their lives for us
Names that will forever last.

What is a name what is a name tell me tell me true
The term by which any person is known
I would like to share mine with you
My name is Verna Hampton
I am an Old Show Girl an OSG
My birthplace is in Boston
I am from Roxbury
I also come from Brooklyn
NYC

I'm a daughter, a sister, and a mother
Both grand and great
And I am here to enlighten, entertain, and educate
What is a name what is a name tell me tell me true
The term by which any person is known to give a name to

Sista FM Diva: The Name Game

People ask me what does FM Diva Mean?
FM always meant Freedom Mouth for me…
And as I further dissected my moniker here is what it be

F. inding
M. yself
D. ealing
I. n
V. irtual
A. merikkka

F. reeing
M. yself by
D. eliberately
I. nteracting with
V. iolent
A. rrogance

F. retting
M. orosely
D. isseminating
I. nformation
V.erifying
A.pocalypse

F. eeling
M. ean,
D. evious,
I. ndifferent,
V. indictive and
A. moral

F. ree
  M. y
    D. evistated
      I. ntelligence
       V. ivisected by
        A. merikkka

And just plain F 'EM!

Araminta

I am Araminta you know me by another name
After years of forced labor and cruelty
I set Me Free
Followed the trails
sheltered in caves
Stayed on the lookout
in the bushes and trees
I set Me Free

I am Araminta
After years of forced labor and cruelty
I crossed over on a boat from shore to shore
And then crossed back again with muffled oar
To set my own family free

I am Araminta
After years of forced labor and cruelty
Patty rollers and dogs would hound my track
on those times that I would traverse forth and back
Going to set my people free
I wanted Us to be as free as Me

I am Araminta, you know me by another name
After years of forced labor and cruelty
The journey was rough and I had to be tough
On the treacherous roads to set Ourselves Free
You will go with me or you will go to your grave
either way, you will no longer be a slave

I am Araminta
After years of forced labor and cruelty
Criminal enslavers put a price tag on my head
It did not matter whether I was alive or dead

26

You see
I did not only assist in setting We,
The chattel that moved their economy, free

I am Araminta
After years of forced labor and cruelty
I was a spy, during the civil war, for their enemy
Fed and nursed the sick and wounded
For the Union Army
1st woman to lead an armed expedition
A strategic and successful war mission
Combahee Ferry
Successfully setting 700, enslaved,
Men, woman, and children Free

I am Araminta
As early as 1852 and maybe before
I lived and worked in Cape May
Studied the routes to freedom during my stay
The home, where I lived, is a museum today
The remnants of a free black community
On the southernmost tip of New Jersey

I am Araminta you know me by another name.

The Mammies In Millie's Window

Walking in New Orleans
Land of magnolias and southern dreams
Walking in New Orleans
In the French Market on Decatur
Walking in New Orleans
Land of crawfish and pecan pralines
Walking in New Orleans
Taking in the city scenes
Striving to be
An unbiased spectator
When towards a little store I came
Millie's just Millie's was the name
Oh how simple and quaint
THEN
I looked in the window and to my surprise
I saw five big black mammies with wide white eyes
Rags on their head and bowls in their hands
Oh the image of the old southland
As I stood there and stared at this stereotypical hypocrisy
I looked to my left and what did I see
Five big fat black men
With chef's hats upon their head
Crisp white aprons on
And lips that were red
Lord have mercy I thought I'd drop dead
It is not the fact that these statues exist
YOU SEE
The original molds
Hold some truths
To my peoples history
I am not ashamed of the work
We were forced to endure
BUT

I was steaming and not screaming
As I walked into that store
What do you have those statues in that window for????
The proprietor sat there quite disengaged
I guess she was Millie, I am really not sure
All I know is
I was really pissed off as I stood by that door
Because they want them she said
With a Cheshire cat shit eating grin
I thought 'count to ten' to myself
As I looked on another shelf
And saw these great big red lips
Pursed for a kiss
THEN I SAID
You mean to tell me
Tourists come in here to buy souvenirs
And you are selling them this!!!
The Mother of Nations
The Queen of the Euphrates and Nile
Her image you mock her throne you defile
WELL
I was ready to scream
I was ready to break
I was ready to give this heifer
A verbal shake
No actually
I was ready to knock that bitch upside her head
BUT
I called on the power of my Sheroes
Took me some pictures
Walked out of that store
And wrote this here poem instead.

Ode to Rosa Parks

She was one of the sparks that ignited
The fuse in our struggle for equality
Her thoughts were on little BoBo that day
The mangled face of the child we knew as Emmitt Till
A false tale of him looking the wrong way
Got him tortured, maimed and killed
His mama, Mamie Till said
"leave the casket open so they won't ever forget what they did to my child"
And I know we never will!
When Ms. Rosa sat down she stood up
For our struggle to be free
A gentle lioness in speech and demeanor
She rattled the worlds' bigots
Who had never even seen her
Our Mother Shero has gone to rest
With the spirits of other ancestors who have shared her quest
Father Crispus Attucks gave his life
In Massachusetts the year 1770
His martyrdom paved the way for freedom
From tyranny for this brand-new country
Mother Sojourner Truth abolitionist and orator
At the age of about seventy
Integrated the streetcars in Washington D.C.
Enslaved freedom fighter Joseph Cinque
Caused mutiny on the high sea
Elizabeth Freeman went into court a slave
And proved that she was free
For forty years after she sat down Ms. Rosa stood up
And taught about the movement for civil rights
The boycotts, the marches, the songs, the speeches, the jails
And the prayers at night
She taught about those who gave their lives for us

And those who fought the good fight

Our gentle giant Rosa Parks
One of the sparks that ignited the fuse
In our fight for equality
When she sat down she stood up
For our struggle to be free.

Michelle's Arms

Michelle's arms
They were on the news this morning
Michelle's arms
They don't wiggle when they wave
Michelle's arms
Lord you know our first lady's charming
She does so many important thangs
But the media mostly talks
Of dress color and bangs
Or how well that jacket hangs
Michelle's arms

Michelle's arms
Grows food in the great lawn garden
Michelle's arms
Comforts parents whose children fell
Michelle's arms
Our first lady is
A health and fitness warden
Sister has a law degree
Can stand up and surmise to a jury
While the media likes to discuss
Is she showing her knees???
Michelle's arms

Michelle's arms
Daughter sister mother wife
Michelle's arms
They ease pain loss and strife
Michelle's arms
The first lady of this land
She is our Sister Queen
Intelligent and so serene

So when you see her on the tv screen
Remember all of her superlative charms
Even if they only
Want to talk about
Michelle's arms

NKC

Nat King Cole
Sang from the soul
His smooth velvet voice
Filling a rhythmic and melodic hole
Long ebony fingers
Expertly flitting up and down the piano keys
When he played and sang
We sat and listened
Hardly able to sit in our seats
We were bobbing our heads
Tapping our feet
Women would swoon
And their knees got weak.
A man of distinction, class and style
His eyes
Looking up from the piano
His full lips
Breaking into that knowing smile
His trio would have you
Dancing and bopping in chairs
On dance floors, in clubs
Up and down the theater aisles and stairs
As his musical acumen and singing fame grew
He was offered a weekly tv show too
November 1956
First Black man, in amerikkka, to achieve this feat
His tv guests were the tops
Singers, musicians, comics, Actors, dancers, comedians
Women, men, black and white
Young and old
Entertainments' cream of the crop
Everyone received their props
The network liked the lineups

Each of his star packed shows did shine
Now, it is said and I agree
That the Nat King Cole show
Was one of the best of its time
But some folks were not happy
And did not want to see
A man who in his face and hue
Embodied Mother Africa on amerikkkan t.v.

Nat King Cole
Had little control
Concerning the image of himself
That Mad Ave. wanted to extol
They brought in the max factor
A color and make up reactor
To erase Africa from his face
And what came next
Made Black people in amerikkka Vexed
The black velvet skin was hidden within
A white blotchy pancake creation
Black skin white mask, was too much to ask
From this gentleman of distinction

Nat King Cole made the choice
To silence his television voice
He chose other realms of stardom
To conquer, rule, and embark
  His truth, spoken back then, stands up to this day
  MADISON AVENUE IS AFRAID OF THE DARK!

The A Word

Question:
What does it mean when the A word is used in a casting breakdown?

The A word?
You know the A word?
THE BIG A
If you don't know you better ask somebody
Let somebody tell ya...
Hi...I am somebody...I'm gonna tell ya
Madison Avenue is still afraid of the dark
A is for Ambiguous
Unclear, uncertain
Unintelligible and vague
Madison Avenue translation
Not to have your motherland stamp on your face.
Not to show a defining feature
Our noses...hair nappy...skin melanated...
Lips beautiful and big
This is a diaspora wide dilemma in my people's case
The case for, not natural, skin that is light
In this millennium gives me a fright
To see the skin lighteners
Pharmaceutical skin brighteners
Popping up all over my world
In a city, village or town
In the hands of
Our little girls
Ebony, Chocolate, Caramel and Sweet Potato Brown
The African Continent, Brazil,
And the Indies East and West
The list of countries is long...
And
Do not forget The U. S.
Diluting the dark hue pallet

To blend in with the rest
Shunning our Motherland beauty
Feeling lighter and brighter
Will bring them the best.
The A Word
The Madison Avenue hype and subliminal dope
When a black girl morphs into a white girl
After using a white bird's soap
That is AMBIGUOUS
Yeah...
Madison Avenue is still afraid of the dark.

How We Feelin' ?!!?

How We Feelin' ?!!?
We sick and tired of being sick and tired of the same ol' same ol'
Our minds and bodies are tired
Of the 400-years of struggle
All types of real struggles
For we people who are of the darker hue

We lost our motherland, our language, our freedom
We fought and died to vote on these shores
No liberties no justice
For Black folks like me and you
We've been lynched, shot and murdered
By white racist supremacy
And by the boys and girls in blue.

How is it that
Now
It is all about "your" feelings and you?
White male guilt and white women crying over their privileges…
Boo F'N Hoo
Because in Beantown
The 46th Presidential election
One out of three
Voted the red and not the blue!

Before we finish Sister FM Diva is going to leave this little nugget with
you…

Black People
You never know which way a cracker's gonna crumble
Til' they fall out of the box
How We Feelin' ?!!?
We will keep our head up

38

We shall continue to do
The same, as we know,
That you will do too...
Use Our Art to Activate Change...Ase

We Out ... All POWER to the PEOPLE!

Written On The A Train Riding Uptown...
The Morning After The Ferguson Verdict

Michael Brown, Michael Brown
They murdered him...they shot him down
On August 9, 2014
Michael Brown, Michael Brown
He was killed in Missouri
The town of Ferguson
Eighteen years old, with his hands in the air, He was Unarmed and he was undone.
When Darren Wilson Murdered Michael Brown with bullets from his policeman's gun
And they declined to charge Darren Wilson for his
Illegal hit...
NOW AIN'T THAT SOME KKK SHIT!!!
As I ride on the A train this morning, on my way uptown
My heart is heavy and my spirit is down
What happened you may ask
What ill to you has been done?
I will tell you my people

THE VERDICT IN FERGUSON

In all of our enslaved years
We have lived with the death and the fears
Racists yelling "get that nigger" ringing in our ears
We did not ask to be here
But here is where we were brought
Sometimes captured and sold by our brothers
And the Europeans bought.
They bought us and they sold us
Breaking our ancestry down
Taking our language and culture
And there has been no rebound

We were force fed another language
Another culture not our own
These evil seeds of the enslaver
Have been hoed and carefully sown
Some of us remain culture free
While they steal and
Appropriate our culture from you and me
Proper education, of self, has never been taught
To those who were sold by those who bought
They robbed us of everything we had
And in return left us with their remnants

Of all things
That are destructive, evil and bad
We imploded on ourselves
Stripped of our Motherland unity
Crime and drugs surging in the community
Making it rain on black butts
And we thinking we are free
Shootin' each other. Yeah we too pull the trigger
And think it is gangsta' to call each other nigger

I do not want you to think that I am getting off track
But I have got to get this 'Ferguson' monkey off of my back
I want you to think of these things that I had to say
And ask yourself on this post Ferguson verdict day
What should I do, what should I say?
Kings and Queens of the universe with the history
and horrors of all the Fergusons
Written upon our face
Do not ever forget
And always
Remember their names
Up ye mighty race

Riding on the A train going uptown
The morning after the Ferguson verdict
After writing this I am not feeling as down
I am not going to let them take my spirit away
I am living proof of our ancestors
And I have a lot to say
A tear starts to trickle down my face
When I see how you have treated our mighty race
Murdering our mothers fathers daughters and sons
Knowing, in full
Black People are the Original ones
I look around on the A train going uptown
And as I see us moving to and fro
I say a special prayer for each one of us
In peace and power go...Ase'

A Seasoned Feeling: Spring Awakening

I feel Winter
Polar winds blowing
Stinging my face
Snow swirling down
Taking up residence on all that is around me
I feel Winter
The cold cold cold
That has me scrunching down
Into my scarf draped neck
To keep the chill abated
I feel Winter
And it was good
Good friends, good food
Good seasonal events
Now Winter is waning
And
I feel Springtime
Coursing through my veins
I feel you
I imagine
Those large hands
That bring life to the earth
Waking up my body's language
With their touch
I feel Springtime
Coursing through my veins
I feel you
I imagine
Being held
Those hands
Playing each note of my body
Passionately
Like you play your mandolin

I feel Springtime
Coursing through my veins
I feel you
I imagine
Your fingers
Brush painting
My body's canvas
Creating a masterpiece
Of modern art strokes
I feel Springtime
Coursing through my veins
I feel you
I Imagine
You
Kissing, caressing, touching
Those special places
Breasts, eyes, toes, ears, throat
The little passenger
In the love boat
I feel springtime
Coursing through my veins
I feel you
I imagine

Why Can't I Write a Poem About Love

I give love
I receive love
I talk about love
Why can't I write a poem about love?
I think about love
I rejoice about love
I lament about love

Why can't I write a poem about love?
I love my family
I love my friends
I can love my man

Why can't I write a poem about love?
I love the smell of spring after an early April morning shower
I love that pair of shoes that makes me bop when I walk
I love a recipe that turns my taste buds up a notch

Why can't I write a poem about love?
I love a vintage Jaguar roadster circa 1960
I love riding the #39 bus over the Williamsburg bridge
I love driving a car on a flat pothole free empty highway road

Why can't I write a poem about love?
I love to perform in front of a Live audience
I love to entertain my friends at my home
I love to attend a good party with interesting people

Why can't I write a poem about love?
I love to trash talk with my Sisterhomegirlfamilyfriends
I love to listen to the elders revisiting
OUR STORY
I love to hear the free and joyous laughter of children at play

Why can't I write a poem about love
I love the Motherland beat of the djembe
I love a good NOLA second line da da da da da
I love Jazz, Blues, R&B, Rock, Reggae, Hip Hop, a Mozart Symphony
Why can't I write a poem about love

Oh… wait a second…never mind…
THIS IS A POEM ABOUT LOVE!

Brown Arms Beating

Brown arms beating, brown arms beating
Brown arms beating the drums
Brown arms beating the rhythms of Mother Africa
Kayaka ka ka....kayaka ka ka....kayaka ka ka ka ka

Brown arms beating brown arms beating,
Brown arms beating the drums
Brown arms beating the drums in Congo Square.
Brown arms beating the drums in Prospect Park
Kayaka ka ka....kayaka ka ka....kayaka ka ka ka ka

Brown arms beating, brown arms beating,
Brown arms beating the drums
Brown arms beating....libations to the ancestors
Brown arms beating....praises to nature
Brown arms beating.... bidding welcome
Kayaka ka ka....kayaka ka ka....kayaka ka ka ka ka

Brown arms, kayaka ka ka
Brown hands kayaka ka ka
Fine brown bodies
Connected to the brown earth
Brown arms beating, brown arms beating, brown arms beating the
drums
Moves my brown frame, moves me, moves me, moves me
When I hear brown arms beating the drums
Kayaka ka ka....kayaka ka ka....kayaka ka ka ka ka kayaka ka ka....
kayaka ka ka....kayaka ka ka ka ka

How Little Louis Learned to Scat: A Jazz Fairytale Poem

Once upon a time long, long ago
In magical New Orleans
There lived in a Magnolia tree a family of birds
They could sing beautiful songs
But sometimes they could not
Remember All of the words

There was also a little boy in New Orleans
Who played the horn
And he always knew the notes when he blew
Little Louis was his name
But when he sang a song
His problem was the same as the birds
Little Louis Could Not Remember All of the Words!

Now Little Louis and the singing birds
They were all friends you see
The school where Little Louis learned to play the horn
Is where the birds lived in a Magnolia tree

One day Little Louis said to his bird friends
What are we to do?
I cannot remember All of the words to my song
And neither can you
.

The birds whistled and jumped around
Fluttering their wings
They told Little Louis they knew
Of only one bird
Who could help them out
With these musical things

Little Louis looked at his friends

And upon his face he wore a scowl
He said Who? Who? Who?
The birds tweeted and chirped
That's right, that's right...The Owl!
She comes to the Magnolia tree
With the moonlight
So you come back here and meet us
When the day has turned into night

WELL...

Little Louis went to the Magnolia tree
When the moon was in the sky
He felt a little nervous
He felt a little shy
But then he felt quite at ease
When he heard the owl gently hoot
Who, who, who, introductions please

The birds made the introductions
His name is Little Louis
And he plays in one of the best bands
That travel all around playing music
In these here magical lands
He is a talented young fella
Little Louis this is the wise young owl
Who is going to help us out
May we introduce you to
Miss Ella

After the introductions
Miss Ella listened to Little Louis and the birds
They told her about their singing

And forgetting some of the words
She answered their question

Without hesitation
Improvise, Improv, Improvisation
Little Louis and the birds asked
What is that?
Miss Ella said
Rockin Robin calls it
SCAT!

When you are singing a song
And if you forget your words
Use a musical note instead
Little Louis and the birds looked at Miss Ella
And they all just shook their head

Miss Ella Owl smiled at them
And then she said
If you don't understand
Please sit down
Fold your wings and fold your hands

Now you listen to me and follow
What I am about to explain
Sing a song whose words
You keep forgetting again and again
Exchange those words

For musical word sounds
Now feel the notes in your mouth
As they go around and around
Little Louis and the birds
Were no longer lost for words

After Miss Ella taught them how to scat
So if you are ever singing under a Magnolia Tree
And you forget your words
Remember
You too can do just that

SCAT!

Thirty Pages
Poetry Inna Mi Yahd…..The Rest Of Mi Place

So this is the next part of mi poetry book'

Mr b say mi don't have nuff words for him to look pon

Mi name doesn't fit on the cover spine

Add thirty more pages he say

Is this book yours?

I thought it was mine

You wait to tell me that

15 days before the book be due

And what…I sposed to feel beholden to you

But why I surprised…when you look in my eyes

And continue to tell the lies

that you have always told

It ain't nothin' new…

it something quite old…..

Page one….you say mi not done

Page eleven... refer to page seven

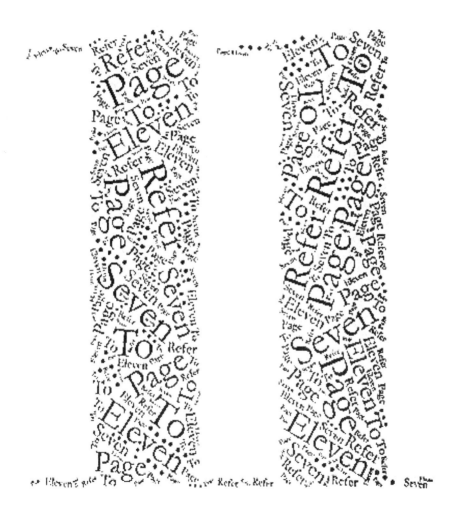

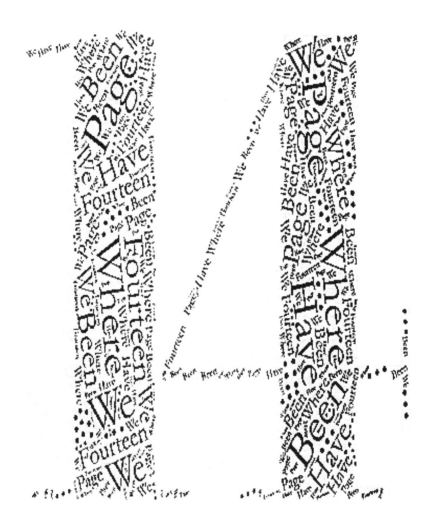

Page fifteen...remaining serene

Page seventeen... they are tryin' to demean

Page nineteen...looking to confuse the Queen

Page twenty-one...no not none

Page twenty-five...know I'm steppin' live

Page twenty-nine...the power is mine

Page thirty...I'll keep it up high,

while you go low down and dirty

Sister FM Diva...Dropping Mike

Acknowledgements: A Public Thanks

A public thanks:

To my ancestors, my family, womentors, mentors, children, grandchildren, cousins, sisters and brothers.
To my friends, the actors, writers, musicians, artists, dancers, and all of the others.
To one thing, two things, you them and another.
To grannies, siblings, fathers, mothers, nieces, uncles, cousins, nephews, and aunts.
Looking over the fertile Maine lands up in the country with Gramps.
To the crushes, boyfriends, the husbands, the lovermen.
And to my foes.
To all of the divas and to all of the devoes.
To my fairy godfather hair stylists. Their finishing school, to strike a pose.
Taught me about high fashion, elan, couture and (how to spot) when a pimp was a pimp and a whore was a whore.
To the mothers and fathers in law, sisters and brothers in law.
To all the in-laws and the out.
And to that extended family folk mix I could go on and on and on about.
To the neighbors, the landlords, and the supers downstairs.
To the live-ins and the flat mates.
To travels international and travels in the states.
To the good times, to the good times, the good times, the good times and those times of strife.
To all of the wisdom that I have gleaned from you.
To the lessons you have taught me in my life.
Thank You, Thank You, Thank You.

Indianapolis, Indiana

Made in the USA
Middletown, DE
09 March 2023